A Garden Wedding

A Garden Wedding

Creating a Lovely Landscape For
Your Ceremony or Reception

by

C.L. Fornari

Paraphyses Press

Paraphyses Press

P.O. Box 355

Osterville, MA 02655

Front cover photo:

The author's entry garden. Photo by C.L. Fornari

Back cover photos:

Father Breck Owens walks daughter Kate Owens down the aisle at her wedding. Photo by Dan Fornari. Other photos by C.L. Fornari

For all who are planning an outdoor wedding

Table of Contents

Introduction

Knowing that there was going to be a wedding in my gardens on September 10th, I spent the early part of the summer planting annuals and sprucing up my property. The perennial borders had been augmented with tall *Nicotiana* that by August were producing hundreds of flowers in several shades of pink. Lilac *Cleome* and white 'Snow Princess' alyssum bordered the area where the ceremony would soon be taking place. Everything was looking full and beautiful…until Hurricane Irene hit Cape Cod on August 28th.

I've been helping other people with such last-minute problems for several years. As a garden consultant I'm frequently called to a property in advance of an upcoming wedding or rehearsal dinner. I assist my clients improve a landscape in advance of the big day. There have also been instances when I've been called in at the eleventh hour to help disguise a visual problem or fix a last minute horticultural disaster.

After doing all the advanced planning and planting for myself, and then dealing with the post-hurricane repair, I now feel even better equipped to offer advice about garden weddings. There is nothing like first hand experience to deepen a person's understanding of the issues at hand.

Even given the hurricane that flattened many annuals and perennials, my gardens looked lovely for the September wedding. My local garden center had the annuals needed to fill in where plants had been leveled, and the three trees that came down provided more branches for the chuppah. Sometimes problems can be turned into blessings.

This experience reinforced my belief that a garden is the perfect location for a wedding, come what may. Since you're reading this book, I know that you're leaning in this direction as well. So let's go into your landscape and explore how to turn your yard into magical surroundings for the big event.

Chapter 1
Location, Location, Location

Well of course you want to hold your wedding or reception in a garden! I may be just a tad biased, but I do think that a garden beats all but the most beautiful churches and for an elegant environment it's leagues above a ballroom, *hands down*. Yes, even if it rains. In all seasons a garden is one of the most life-affirming places on earth. You have definitely chosen the perfect location.

There are the obvious practical considerations, of course, and that's what we'll cover in this chapter. After

3

that we'll get to the fun stuff like flowers, paper lanterns, flowers, arbors, and did I mention flowers? But before we talk about the blooming plants, a word about the location. You'll want to evaluate the property with clear eyes, a pen and paper or smart phone, and the checklist at the end of this chapter.

Timing is Everything

Start with the area where the ceremony will be held, being sure to spend time in the garden during the same hours your gathering will take place. The yard that is delightful in the early morning might be as hot as the Sahara desert once it's exposed to the afternoon sun. Similarly, the garden that looks so charming during the day might become as dark as a cave once evening sets in.

Not that these situations are impossible to deal with: you can hope for a cloudy day, rent a tent for shade, or plan for an evening wedding in the hot garden. Stringing lights and adding candles in a space that proves to be dark is fairly easy as well, but in any case you need to be prepared.

Being in the garden at the same time and season when the wedding will take place will also inform you about where the sun is at that hour. The bride and groom shouldn't be squinting or forced to wear sunglasses to avoid solar glare. It might just be a matter of starting the wedding a few minutes later so that the sun's position will have moved. It's a good idea to make notes about where the sun is going to be during the wedding. It's also helpful to take some snapshots so you can remember where the sunlight and shadows fall. Your photographer may have an opinion about this as well.

Try to also visit the garden on a rainy day remembering that inclement weather doesn't have to ruin a garden wedding. However, if the area where the bride will enter becomes flooded every time it rains, it's best to know about it well in advance so you can fix the situation.

Think about where your guests can sit or stand without looking directly into the sun at the time of the ceremony. If the wedding or party will take place after dark, observing the garden at that hour can reveal where you'll need supplemental lighting. Don't wait for the dress rehearsal to discover how the garden will function for the wedding party and attendees. Instead, walk through the property several times – first pretending you're a guest and then again while imagining you're the bride and bridal party.

When planning the preparation of the gardens for a ceremony or reception, you'll evaluate what the property already looks like and what will need to be done before the event. Doing this in an organized way is essential if you don't want to drive yourself and everyone concerned absolutely crazy.

Using this book, a notebook, or a laptop, begin by filling out the following checklist.

☐ How many guests will be attending, and is there room for all of them?

☐ Where will the cars be parked, and is it possible for people of all ages to get to where the ceremony will be held?

☐ Are there any local zoning laws or neighborhood regulations that will affect the parking or party?

☐ Will there be a tent in case it rains, and if so, where will it be erected? Has the tent rental company given their approval to the site?

☐ Where will photographs be taken? Are there already places in the garden that would make a good background for the pictures of family and the bridal party, or do these sites need to be created?

☐ Where will the bride and groom stand during the ceremony? Where will they enter the garden?

☐ Are there existing arbors or other structures that can be used? Will there be a focal point or chuppah?

☐ Will there be musicians or a DJ, and where will they be located?

☐ Will there be a reception after the ceremony, and if so, where will the cocktails/bar be located and the food served?

☐ If there is a single tent for both the ceremony and reception, where will the guests go while the tables are being set up?

☐ If the caterer needs access to a cook tent or van, where might these be located?

☐ Will there be musicians for the wedding ceremony itself, and do they need a source of electricity?

☐ Where are the outlets for lights, catering equipment, and the musicians? Will the existing power sources support all the equipment needed without tripping circuit breakers or blowing fuses? If not, where can a generator be placed?

☐ Will you rent Porta-Potties, and if so, where will they be located?

☐ In addition to what will be blooming in the garden, where will additional bouquets or pots of flowers be positioned? (Note: this is something that may evolve over time – just keep it in mind as you survey the garden for now.)

☐ Which gardens/plants will be most visible to guests?

☐ Which gardens/plants will be in the background of the ceremony itself?

☐ Which areas will be most visible during cocktail hour and/or the reception?

☐ As you survey the garden in advance, which areas immediately strike you as needing improvement?

Chapter 2
Long-Range Planning

Once you know where the ceremony will take place
and which plantings will be the most visible, it's time to
decide how much improvement these gardens will need.
Since many plants take some time to mature, it would be
advisable to put additional shrubs and perennials in place
as far in advance as possible. This will allow them time to
get well established and grow larger.

Although it might be desirable to use plants that will be in bloom for the wedding, it's not always possible. If the season is extremely hot, dry, wet, or cool, the weather will influence when shrubs and perennials bloom and how long they stay in flower. So even if you're adding flowering shrubs and perennials, it's also wise to leave space in all of your beds for annual flowering plants. These can be put in place at any time, from one week to three months before the big day.

Planting Shrubs and Trees

Planning a wedding around the blooming of specific plants can be tricky. You might have always dreamed of getting married when the lilacs that your grandmother planted are in bloom, for example, but the timing might be problematic. In general, spring blooming trees and shrubs stay in bloom for shorter periods. Lilacs, for example, flower for about two to three weeks.

On the other hand, some summer-flowering plants such as hydrangeas can bloom for months. The longer the typical flowering period is, the better the chance of having that plant in bloom for the wedding. This isn't to say you should forget your dream of saying "I do" under Grandma's lilacs. It's just to mention that everyone should keep a certain degree of flexibility when it comes to the natural world.

Once the date has been set you can start evaluating existing plants and begin putting new ones in the ground. Check with local nurseries, cooperative extensions, and garden radio hosts about which shrubs and perennials are likely to be in bloom on the big day. These are good resources for helping you choose what to plant. Varieties that will grow large can be planted singly, but smaller shrubs and perennials make a better show if they're grouped in clusters of three, five, or seven. Odd numbers are always more appealing to the human eye.

In all but the most formal gardens, staggering the plants rather than putting them in straight lines makes for a more attractive garden. Planting in "puddles" instead of lines is also smart because if one or two plants die the entire design isn't ruined.

Although many people automatically think of using plants with white flowers as a backdrop for a wedding, there are a couple of reasons that an all white garden isn't the best idea. First of all, white flowers show browned edges as they start to fade. This makes them less attractive as the blooms go by; the larger the flower, the more noticeable the browning will be.

If the season is unusually warm, white flowering shrubs will bloom earlier and wilt faster and the browned petals can create an unattractive background for the ceremony. The Queen in *Alice and Wonderland* might have been able to paint her roses red, but it's pretty hard to make browned flowers look white again.

In addition, white flowers are harder to photograph and don't make as nice a background for a bride in a white dress. So instead of instantly gravitating toward all white flowers, consider brighter colors or a mix of some white along with other hues. If the bride has picked her favorite shades for bridesmaids' dresses and other decor, you could use plants with complimentary flowers.

If you're uncertain about which direction the wedding colors will go, know that lavender, pale yellow, peach, and light green flowers compliment most other colors. Plants with these hues shouldn't clash with other colors that the wedding party chooses.

Diversity is always a smart strategy in the garden, and when planning for an event it's even more important.

Instead of planting an entire yard full of one type of flowering plant, use at least three. This will help insure a beautiful setting on the big day. In other words, if insects, disease, or high winds happen to destroy a particular plant type, it's likely that the others will remain.

Planting Perennials

I've done several garden consultations that have been scheduled a year in advance of the event. All of the homeowners have asked me the same question, "What perennials can I plant this year that will be in bloom for the wedding?" My response has always been, "Not so fast…"

Timing the flowering of perennials is similar to timing the bloom of shrubs: it's uncertain at best. First of all, some perennials bloom longer than others. Second, a particularly warm or cold season will delay or accelerate periods of bloom. Third, if you're buying perennials a year in advance, know that garden centers frequently stock plants that are blooming earlier or later than their normal bloom time. These plants are typically grown in other areas and shipped in. Plants in bloom in the garden center in, say, June or July, may or may not be flowering at the same time the following year. For these reasons, planting perennials a year in advance expecting that they'll be in flower on a particular date is chancy.

That said, there are some perennials that bloom for long periods of time, making it more likely that they'll be flowering for the wedding. Keep in mind, however, that blooming times vary from region to region; what may be a long bloomer in cool climates might come and go quickly in hot weather. Ask for recommendations at a local garden center or cooperative extension instead of relying on a list from the Internet, unless the website you're consulting is specific to your region.

Nourish the Turf

If the ceremony will be held on a lawn, care should be taken to build up the strength of the grass well in advance. Top-dress thin areas with topsoil and scatter grass seed to fill in bare places. In northern areas where cool season grasses are grown, mow the lawn at three inches high all season in order to leave enough leaf surfaces to build energy in the plants.

In the southern United States where Bermuda grass is frequently the lawn of choice, mow at an inch tall. St. Augustine grass, another popular turf grass in southern states, should be mowed between 1 to 3 inches in height.

Any major seeding should be done in either the fall or spring before the wedding. If done in the fall, the plants will be strong and more mature for an event the following year. Fertilize the lawn in the spring and fall using an organic fertilizer. Whether you've reseeded or not, top-dressing with compost works like magic to create thicker, greener turf. Do this at least seven months before the wedding. This gives plenty of time for populations of beneficial micro-organisms to build in the soil.

Water lawns deeply but less often, and don't be tempted to set automatic sprinkler systems to water every day. Too much moisture is a contributing factor to every lawn disease, not to mention moss growth. When you water deeply the turf develops deep roots, but the surface of the soil dries up. This makes the conditions less hospitable to fungi and other pathogens.

If pets are accustomed to using the lawn to "do their business," be sure to spend time training them to use another area. It's best to do this the year before the wedding, if possible. Dog urine can cause brown or highly green patches on the lawn, and no one wants to step in dog feces on the day of the wedding.

Animal Control

If animals are using your lawn for a toilet, there are ways to train them to go elsewhere — even if they aren't your animals. The Scarecrow, made by Contech, and the Spray Away, from Havahart, are motion activated sprinklers that produce a hard and sudden spray of water when an animal walks in front of them. These products are effective for teaching neighborhood dogs or cats to avoid your lawn; they're also useful for keeping geese, digging skunks, and grazing deer away. Find out more about the Scarecrow at www.contech-inc.com and learn about the Spray Away at www.havahart.com.

Install motion activated sprinklers or other animal deterrents well before the wedding, allowing plenty of time for critters to learn to go elsewhere. For better or worse, animals are creatures of habit. Getting rid of problem critters is often a matter of forcing them to break their routines and develop new ones.

Don't be tempted to spread mothballs in an attempt to repel animals; this doesn't work and you never know where the balls will end up. I've seen a crow pick up a mothball from a neighbor's yard and fly away with it. I worry that the bird might have dropped it where a child could have picked it up. Mothballs don't especially bother animals, and they are fairly toxic, so they're best reserved for indoor, moth-repelling jobs.

Permanent Structures

If you've always dreamed of getting married in a gazebo, or beneath an arbor, install such structures as soon as possible. There will be damage to the lawn or surrounding gardens during the construction or installation, so the sooner you can reseed turf and restore flowerbeds the better.

Be realistic about the plantings you envision growing on and over these structures. Unless you start three or four years in advance, it's unlikely that you'll have an arbor dripping with roses or a gazebo covered with shady vines. If the wedding is at the end of summer or fall however, you might be able to grow annual vines such as morning glories that will fill a large area in one season.

When planning for annual vines, be sure that your structure receives at least six hours of full sun because that is the amount of light most of these plants require. Another key to success in getting rapid development of annual vines is advanced preparation of the soil. Amending the soil with compost or composted manure and digging this in a wide, deep area is a key to fast growth.

Just because the roses or honeysuckle won't fill the arbor in one summer doesn't mean that you can't have something colorful or celebratory for the wedding. Structures can always be planted with the best plants for the long-term life of the garden and then decorated with fresh flowers, tiny lights, or bells just before the event. See more about structures in chapter 7.

Fencing is another structure to consider adding before a wedding. Some wish to screen the view to a street or neighbor's property, and others want to hide air conditioners or other utilities. Like arbors, pergolas, or gazebos, the earlier these are put in place the better.

Many localities have zoning regulations or other laws about the size and placement of permanent structures. In some cases fences can only be so high, utility box screening must be so far from the meters, and gazebos or sheds only so close to property lines. Before you go ahead with any building or installation, be sure to check with your local building inspector about such laws.

A Visit to the Garden Center

Even when planning a year in advance, it's not too early to go to the garden center. Once the wedding date is set, head over to your local nursery and talk with the manager who does the ordering. Ask which plants they are likely to have in stock two weeks before your wedding date and if it's possible to place special orders at that time of year. This will give you a better idea of which plants might be purchased at the last minute and which ones will need to be placed in the landscape well in advance.

Some garden centers sell flowering annuals late into the season and others close down after the Fourth of July, so it's smart to understand your last minute options well in advance. For example, knowing that your garden center doesn't offer much after mid July, you might want to plant up large pots of annuals yourself so you have plenty of these on hand.

In chapters 5 and 6 I discuss some of the many options for adding flowers to the garden, in preparation for the wedding. Depending on the date of the event, some of these may need to be planted two or more months before the party. If you want a garden ringed with pale pink impatiens, for example, and the wedding date is in late August or early September, those annuals will need to be planted in the spring or early summer.

You'll find a series of questions listed below, toward the bottom of the long-range checklist. Take this list of questions to your local garden center as soon as you know the date of your wedding.

Long-Range Checklist

☐ I need to plant shrubs and trees before the wedding.
List locations:

☐ I need to plant perennials. List the locations:

☐ I need to improve the lawn.

☐ I want to put in some permanent structures. List
which structures you want to build and where they will be
located:

☐ When I visit my local garden center I need to ask the
following questions:
1.   If my wedding date is _____, are you likely to
have any pots of annuals or hanging baskets of flowering
annuals for sale at that time of year?

2.   What type of annuals are you likely to have three or
four weeks before my wedding date?

3.　What colors are the annuals that are typically available around that date?

4.　If I want several pots of annuals or hanging baskets that are all the same color, will I need to order them in advance?

5.　If we need to order plants, when does that order need to be placed?　What happens if the grower is out of what I want…do you have alternate sources you can turn to?

6.　If I need to plant annuals well in advance of my wedding date, which ones will last the best in this area? Note: Be sure to go into the garden center knowing if you're looking for plants that do well in sunny areas or shady areas (or both). The nursery staff will need to know this in order to advise you correctly.

7.　Will this garden center do custom planting of containers and deliver them to our house? Do you have anyone who will come to the property and fill pots and boxes for me? How far in advance do we need to plan?

Chapter 3
Short-Range Planning

The Wedding's This Month!

Whether you've been planning your wedding for a year or more, or you've just decided that you're going to get married in the garden next week, there are eleventh-hour things you can do to improve the garden.

Last Minute Cleanup

The first thing to do is to walk around the garden several times, focusing on different things each time through. On the first walk focus on your feet. Are there rough places that should be smoothed, driveways or patios that need sweeping, or muddy patches that could be covered with boardwalks or stepping-stones? Are there any spots where people might not see a stone, step, or other tripping hazard?

Make a list of any passageways that need to be quickly cleaned, covered, or blocked off in some manner in order to make walking convenient and safe.

Second, walk around the yard and look for dead wood or failing plants. These are easy to overlook, but they'll show up in photographs later – detracting from the rest of the garden and the bride and groom. Any branches that are brown or wilted should be cut away from otherwise healthy plants; any dead plants should be removed completely.

Last Minute Flowers

Next, walk around looking for the logical places where flowers would improve the garden. Start a list estimating the number of plants needed so that you can take this to the garden center. Be realistic about how much time there is for planting and possible mulching of beds.

Keep in mind that flowering plants don't necessarily have to be planted in the ground. If the pots are attractive or unobtrusive, they can either be placed on top of the soil or dug in just enough to prevent them from tipping over.

Clay, wood, or metal containers can also disguise plastic pots. If these aren't heavy they should be sunk three or four inches into the ground so that they'll stand up to gusts of wind. Plan to put these decorative containers in place several days before the wedding but keep the plastic potted flowering plants in another location. This will allow you to water the potted plants efficiently. The plastic pots can be popped into their containers the day before the wedding.

Some garden centers will rent plants for a day or two. This might be something to explore if you want a colorful background for the ceremony but have a limited budget. In such cases the plants are usually picked up or delivered the day before the event and returned the day after. Using decorative containers to disguise plastic nursery pots, as described above, is a good way to keep borrowed plants stable, attractive, and in good shape.

Should such rented plants be damaged and made unsalable you'd need to pay for them. When borrowing plants make sure that they are secure and not in locations where they might be crushed. Similarly, when renting large pots or urns of flowering plants be sure not to place them near the bar area. It's common for people to dump unwanted beverages into a potted plant without realizing that alcoholic drinks and hot coffee can injure or kill the plants.

When it comes to flowers, more is more. Groups make a bigger statement than one plant here and another there. For example, if you have budgeted for the purchase of twelve plants, it would be better to buy either all twelve the same type and color or two groups of six that are the same. In either case, these can be placed as groups of three in the landscape. This will look better than using one or two of many assorted varieties.

If you think the garden would look neater if the beds are mulched, be sure to plant any flowers before the mulch is laid down. Use dark brown mulch such as shredded pine bark. The orange or black "color enhanced" products might predominate in photos and detract from the flowers.

The Lawn

One month before the wedding is too late to repair the lawn unless sod is used. You can lay sod a month before the event. However, installing it any closer to the date of the event will likely result in the destruction of the turf from foot traffic. Be sure that any new sod strips are laid close together so the seams don't create tripping hazards for the wedding party or guests.

Water all turf deeply and regularly, but not too often. A deep soaking less often is better than a little water every day. Once a week in cool temperatures, and twice a week when sunny days are over 85 degrees should be sufficient. If the daily temperatures soar to over 95 degrees, every other day soakings may be needed. This will depend on the type of grass you have and the climate where you live. Always be sure to get local advice from a turf expert.

Plan to soak the lawn well two or three days before the event, but *don't water the day of the wedding.* Wet soil compacts more easily, so all of those feet walking on a newly watered lawn will do more damage than the same traffic on a drier surface.

Keeping the soil on the dry side will be a gift to the women who wear high heels. Dry soil will support such footwear better so that guests are less likely to sink or trip.

A Final Top-Dressing

After all the flowering plants are installed, the final step in your last minute sprucing up might be to apply a layer of bark mulch over any visible open ground. This will neaten the property and provide a unifying look to the most prominent beds.

Common bark mulch is better than cocoa or buckwheat hulls, especially in places where it can be windy. Hulls are lightweight and will blow around the property given a stiff breeze. You want the bride to be showered with rice or flower petals *after* the wedding, not pelted with hulls before the ceremony. Additionally, cocoa hulls smell chocolaty when dry but they can stink to high heaven after they've been wet for a while. Stick to plain bark mulch and you won't have to worry about these problems.

Insect Control

Another task on your last minute list will be mosquito or insect control. This doesn't mean fogging the entire property with hazardous insecticides. Fortunately there are organic and least-toxic products that are very effective.

Most of these insect and mosquito repellants are odor based, so they are best applied in advance. Since the odor from many mosquito repellants is detectable by humans for the first twelve to twenty-four hours, it's best not to apply these products on the day of the wedding itself. Some products recommend an application two or more days before maximum control is needed, while others should be put down within twenty-four hours of the event. Be sure to read labels and follow the directions.

Mosquito repellants are usually available at local garden centers, but should your retail outlets not carry them they can be ordered from the Internet. Companies such as Gardener's Supply carry repellants that are highly effective.

Hiring Help

When evaluating all that needs to be done in the month before a wedding, some people decide that they need assistance. Hiring a consultant, professional gardener, or landscaping crew might make it all less overwhelming. Even having someone who will water potted or newly planted annuals, or complete a little last minute weeding, can be a tremendous relief.

A word of caution in this regard, however; unless you've worked with the gardener or landscapers in the past, make sure you're at home when they're working on your property. They might be the most professional, competent workers on the planet, but that doesn't mean they necessarily share your sensibility about how the garden should look for the wedding.

Given the charge to "clean things up before next weekend," one person might think this means raking up fallen leaves and mulching beds while another might imagine you want all the shrubs chopped in half and sheared into round, green meatballs. Believe me, it's happened.

Give anyone who is helping you a detailed list in writing, and then keep an eye on their progress as they work. This is not to say that you can't trust your gardener or landscapers. It's just good to be reminded that even when we think we've been clear about what we want, there may be other ways to interpret what we've written or said. Don't assume anything, especially a week before the wedding.

Short-Range Checklist

☐ Clean-up, raking and removal of deadwood is needed here:

☐ After viewing the gardens from where the guests will be entering, seated during the ceremony, standing for cocktails and walking to the reception, make the following list. I need to plant annuals for flower color in the following places:

☐ Mulch as top-dressing needed here:

☐ The following areas need to be hidden using large potted plants or bamboo screening:

☐ The chuppah or arch should be constructed on this day:

☐ The lawn needs to be mowed on this day:

☐ Remember to water any and all potted plants the week before the wedding *and* on the morning of the event itself.

☐ Put pots of flowers in place either the day before the event or the morning of the ceremony.

☐ Consider using large pots of flowers to help direct people where you want them to go. Containers can block access to the driveway, storage areas or walkways. List such areas where large pots or urns are needed:

Chapter 4
Problem Plants and Other Eyesores

I Never Noticed These Were *Ugly*...

When planning for an event taking place in the landscape, we quickly begin to see everything with new eyes. Those sheared shrubs that have thin green tops and bare stems suddenly look like oddly formed, living coffee tables instead of foundation plantings. The partly browned evergreen that's out by the street now appears more dead than alive, and the large shrub you've walked around for years is now visible for what it truly is: *way* overgrown.

How such eyesores are dealt with depends on when the wedding is scheduled. If there is sufficient time to remove them and plant something else in the same location, that's probably the best solution. If the wedding is just around the corner and the last thing you need is a trip to the garden center to shop for shrubs, then consider a touchup job instead.

Removing any and all dead leaves and stems will immediately improve most ugly plants. Be sure not to make any cuts that leave bare stumps, however. Cut dead limbs all the way back to one inch from the trunk and take away all dead foliage. Do this for both trees and shrubs.

If the plant looks worse once this is done, you know it's time to cut bait completely. Ugly shrubs can always be cut off at ground level and the stump covered with a thin layer of mulch. If doing this creates a large space you can easily fill the area. You might group three or more large pots planted with flowering annuals, or even use a birdbath or other garden ornaments to fill the spot.

Benches can also be used to attractively fill large spaces – even in places such as foundation beds where it isn't the norm to have a bench. These can actually be a pleasing way to transform a gap into an area for rest.

In the face of an overgrown landscape, some might decide to cut their shrubs back *hard*. This is the Marine Corps barber approach. This type of renovation pruning can sometimes be effective, but it's more likely to create butchered looking plants for the short term. Cleaning up larger, overgrown shrubs by pruning from the ground up, or by simply removing dead growth may be the percentage play – especially if you're close to the wedding date.

Fresh cuts are always more noticeable on shrubs and trees as well, so for many reasons it's probably wise not to do any major pruning right before the event.

Everything is *Green*

Looking at your yard as the location for a wedding, you might notice that you have a good amount of green foliage but not much else. Some properties are filled with serviceable evergreens and not many flowers; others have plants in bloom, but only at certain times of the year.

Here's the good news: all of those green plants make a great background for photos of the wedding party. More good news: adding flowers for the big day is relatively easy. Landscaping that's composed of green foliage isn't a problem as long as those plants are looking their best. If the plants are healthy and all dead wood or dried leaves have been removed, just tend to those in need of trimming and you're over halfway there. Various ways to add more flowers are discussed in chapter 5.

It Just Died!

It happens: two weeks before a big event the small tree that has been a focal point next to the driveway suddenly turns brown and sheds all its leaves. Maybe you're at the end of a long dry spell, the tree was attacked by a fungus, or some well meaning person over fertilized.

Diagnosing the cause is almost beside the point. A plant has died and you need to decide what to do about it as quickly as possible. There are a couple of quick fixes for situations like this. The first involves speedy removal and the second uses the old lemons into lemonade strategy.

If the plant that suddenly departed for plant heaven isn't very large, the best solution might be to cut it down and have it hauled away. Be sure that any stump or stem is cut right to ground level. This makes it easier to hide and prevents any remnants from becoming tripping hazards.

On the other hand, when a large tree suddenly dies there may not be time to cut it down – especially because doing so can disrupt the landscaping around the dead plant. It's almost better to leave a dead tree in place than to have the lawn strewn with fresh tire ruts and sawdust on the day of the wedding. Besides, dead trees can be decorated and made into a garden asset. I once had a small tree die a couple of weeks before a garden tour. My property was part of the event, so I had to get creative. I painted the tree bright blue and it was the hit of the tour.

Larger trees can be more difficult to cover with color, but they can be wound with strings of white fairy lights, or used to hang large, white paper lanterns. The skeletons of dead shrubs or trees can also be used to display origami birds, paper flowers, ribbons, banners, or other ornaments appropriate to the season or wedding theme. Treat dead trees as if they are structures for your décor, not deceased plants.

Although a deceased tree can be turned into something decorative, dead shrubs or lifeless smaller plants should probably be removed. If there isn't time, don't worry about digging the plant completely out of the soil. Cut it down to ground level and throw it away.

Meters, Hoses, and Poison Ivy

When the eyesore is a group of meters, air conditioners, or other equipment, it's not possible to haul them off or decorate them with lights or paper birds. These visual problems are usually best hidden by fences or folding screens, not plants. Screening can either be permanent, as in a fence that's installed before the wedding and left in place, or it can be temporary.

Bamboo or reed window shades are a great choice for temporary screening. They are often sold in discount or big-box stores. To install these shades as screening pound stakes into the ground and tie or staple the shades to the supports. When used as window coverings, the bamboo or reeds span horizontally across the glass. For use as screening, however, make sure to place the blinds so that the reeds run vertically. The reeds will then stand upright at the right height and you'll be able to wrap them around what you need to screen.

The key to getting the temporary screening to look good is to make sure the tops of the stakes don't stick up behind the top of the screen. Also make sure the screening is tied or fastened well to the supporting stakes. Sagging dividers can actually call more attention to problems rather than hide them.

Bamboo or reed window blinds can be quickly painted with fast drying latex paint as well. The blinds are typically a tan color, so if grey, white, or another color would blend better with your house then by all means take out a roller and paint them.

Another creative screening is to take wooden shutters and fasten the edges together with hinges so they zigzag to form a freestanding partition. Old wooden shutters are often listed in the "Free" section of Craigslist, so check your local classifieds to see what's available.

If a tall screen is needed, the louvered wooden closet doors sold at home centers can be made into the same sort of zigzag using hinges. These doors are six or more feet high; when purchased unfinished they're not very expensive. However, keep in mind that painting them can be time consuming because of the numerous wooden slats.

Premade screens for blocking air conditioners or other utilities can be purchased at home stores or through mail order. An online search for "outdoor screen enclosure" brings up several options.

In addition to equipment or other items that need hiding, you might notice places where the house itself needs attention. Chipped paint or rotten wood, for example, might suddenly stand out. It's always possible to repair these areas before the wedding. But should you decide that a total fix up isn't in the budget, know that you'll see these things far more readily than anyone else will. A happy bride and groom in a pretty garden will have everyone's attention. The guests will be unlikely to notice the flaking paint.

No amount of screening or visual distraction can cover up hazardous situations, however. You may be aware of that large patch of poison ivy next to the lawn and take care to avoid it, but you can be sure that this is exactly where a wedding guest will drop something or fall down. You may know to stay away from the rotted wood on the well cover, or the really wobbly fence, but your guests can't be expected to either know or remember such perilous locations. These unsafe conditions should be fixed well in advance of the wedding.

Hire a professional to remove poison ivy, poison oak, or sumac and have rotted trees, fences, or other unstable structures removed and replaced.

Chapter 5
Flowers, Flowers, Flowers

The Plants You Have

As I mentioned in chapter 2, since we can't control the weather it's perilous to plant shrubs and perennials in advance of the wedding and then assume they'll be in bloom for the event. Unusually hot, cold, wet or dry seasons can alter even the most reliable of bloom times.

That said, there are some things you can do to ensure that those plants are more likely to be in flower. First of all, don't under or over water your plants. I'll repeat myself on this important point: a deep soaking less often is better than a little water every day. You want to be sure that your plants are healthy so the flowers don't dry out or rot. In general, it's best to water for over an hour, every four or five days. This is far preferable than watering daily for fifteen minutes.

Second, don't fertilize your shrubs or perennials much, especially right before the wedding. An application of a general, organic fertilizer in the spring is fine, but don't apply synthetic fertilizers right before the wedding. Doing so increases the danger of burning your plants. If the flowers aren't open because the season has been cool, synthetic fertilizer won't hurry them along. In fact, it might actually cause the buds to drop.

Finally, all is not lost if the flowers have gone by on the plants you were counting on. Simply pick the browned or wilted blossoms off to make the plant look cleaner. You can always add more color using some last minute annuals.

Annuals

When it comes to adding flowers to your yard or turning a run-of-the-mill landscape into a *garden*, you can't beat annuals. Yes, they'll only live for one season, but many of them bloom for months with little care other than watering – and you can't top them for flower power. When you put your annuals in the ground will depend on where you live and the date of the wedding.

If the wedding is in July, August or September, plant young annuals in late spring or early summer, after the typical last frost date in your area. Call your local garden center if you're unsure of this date because it can vary from region to region.

The following is a list of annuals that are reliable and long blooming, both in the cooler northern regions and hotter southern climates. Some of these plants are commonly available in six packs and others are usually sold in small pots.

Before you go plant shopping, make sure to check and see how much sun your gardens receive. Full sun means that the area gets direct, uninterrupted sunshine for at least six hours a day, including the noon hour. Most full sun plants will do well if they get at least four hours of sun, including mid-day when the sun is strongest.

Part shade means the plants receive four hours of sun in the early morning or late afternoon, or some combination of these times. If you have gardens that are sunny from eight in the morning to just before noon, for example, this would be a part shade garden. In this case you'd be better off using shade plants.

Full shade is an area that gets no direct sun at all, or perhaps just a few hours of dappled sun through a canopy of trees.

Tips for Success with Annuals

Place your annuals in groups around shrubbery or trees, or in spaces between perennials. If you plant your annuals around established plants, be sure to loosen the surrounding soil and mix in some slow-release fertilizer.

For annuals, I'm especially partial to using a mix of a slow-release fertilizer combined with an organic product. If you prefer all organic fertilizers, however, mix in a granular product when you loosen the soil, along with some compost or composted manure. Then fertilize with a liquid such as fish and seaweed emulsion; do this the second week after planting. This will help to jump-start your plants. The nutrients in the liquid should be more readily available to the plants and the granular product will kick in later in the season.

Be sure not to over fertilize in your effort to make the plants grow quickly. Too much fertilizer can kill your plants or make them grow too tall and weak. You don't want to have floppy annuals that blow over or get beaten down by rainfall before the wedding.

Young plants will need watering more frequently than established ones. Water every two or three days at first and then taper down to longer soakings less often. Remember that it's good to let the surface of the soil dry between sprinklings; if you've soaked the soil deeply, the roots will still be moist, even as the surface dries.

Annuals for Sun and Part Sun

Spider Flower (*Cleome hassleriana*) Medium to tall in height, these plants are available in pink, white, and purple forms. Plant them in the back of the border and keep the foliage away from where people walk – the leaves smell a bit like skunk spray. *Cleome* is nice as a cut flower as well as a landscape plant. But here's a word of warning if your event is later in the summer: with the exception of the variety called Senorita Rosalita, this annual gets bare on the bottom by late summer. When planted among other flowers that are under two feet tall this isn't a problem, but when used in groupings of just *Cleome* alone, the bare legs aren't very attractive. Plant Senorita Rosalita for a long-lasting, full *Cleome*.

Cosmos (*Cosmos* species) Round flowers in shades of pink and white cover medium to tall plants. The taller varieties might need staking. Cosmos are most striking in bloom in late summer to early fall, so don't use them for early color.

Dahlias (*Dahlia* hybrids) For central and northern gardens, dahlias are the queens of the garden from August until hard frost. In hot and humid climates you'll want to plant them in morning sun and afternoon shade. In either case, they are colorful and one of the best plants for cutting gardens. Many are tall and need staking, so read about the tubers or plants you're buying to make sure you place them appropriately. You'll find the best selection of dahlias if you purchase tubers or cuttings in the spring.

Zinnia (*Zinnia* species) Natives of Mexico, these annuals like sun and heat. They are not the annual of choice if you have an automatic irrigation system or frequent rainfall, however. New cultivars such as the Profusion series make better border and landscape plants because of their compact nature and repeat blooming, so look for this compact variety for gardens. For cutting, plant taller varieties such as Berry Basket, Blue Point, Cut and Come Again, California Giant, and State Fair mix.

Starflower (*Pentas lanceolata*) *Pentas* are perfect for adding color to any sunny garden and do well in hot climates. They mix well with perennials and attract hummingbirds and butterflies. Clip off the spent flowers through the summer for faster and better repeat blooms.

Dusty Miller (*Senecio cineraria*) For those who like silver foliage, dusty miller is a must. This is a particularly nice plant to use in areas where people will gather in the evening since the foliage will show up in the dark. For the best effect, however, plant dusty miller in groups of seven or more and repeat those groups in several places around the garden. One plant here and there will just look a bit like polka dots. Dusty miller can also make an attractive border when planted in a row around an entire bed.

Globe Amaranth (*Gomphrena globosa*) If you live in an area where summers are hot, this is a good annual for your garden. The flowers are small, round balls of color, spread over the plant. The plants themselves are medium in height. Newer varieties such as Fireworks are tall, brightly colored, and extremely tolerant of hot weather.

Fan Flower (*Scaevola aemula*) *Scaevola* gets my vote for the easiest, most versatile annual for sunny gardens. It's great in the ground or when it's cascading over the edge of containers. The blue varieties are more vigorous than the white, and the foliage of all cultivars is a fresh bright green. I've seen fan flower do well in cool, rainy summers and hot, dry conditions alike.

Purple Heart (*Setcreasea pallida)* If you love purple, combine the fan flower above with some purple heart and smile all summer. *Setcreasea* has rich purple leaves and small lavender flowers: two for one! It adds depth, color, and interest to containers or the front of flower gardens and it mingles well with alyssum, *Scaevola*, and *Verbena*.

Creeping Zinnia (*Sanvitalia procumbens*) This is almost a groundcover annual with dark green foliage and small yellow flowers. Although the flowers aren't large, they are bright yellow and numerous. *Sanvitalia* mixes well with *Scaevola* and Snow Princess alyssum for a classic yellow, white, and blue combination.

Gold Medallion (*Melampoddium paludosum*) Yellow daisy-like flowers cover the bright green foliage on this low, shrubby annual. This is another good choice for hot climates, but be sure to plant it early in the season.

Mexican Heather (*Cuphea hyssopifolia*) Although the flowers on this *Cuphea* aren't large, they are abundant and the plant is reliable and neat. Use Mexican Heather in the front of flowerbeds or in boxes and containers. This plant makes a nice textural contrast for annuals that have large leaves and flowers. You can find varieties of Mexican heather with magenta, pink, or white flowers.

'Blue Horizon' Ageratum (*Agerautm houstonianum*) Although 'Blue Horizon' is taller than most varieties of Ageratum sold, I happen to think that it's the most reliable for summer-into-fall flowering. 'Blue Horizon' grows between two to three feet tall and benefits from a deadheading session in mid-summer. This annual does best in northern gardens as it is not especially heat or drought tolerant. It is, however, a must for the cutting garden and the perfect companion for zinnias.

Snow Princess Alyssum (*Lobularia* hybrid) This is one of the best new plants I've grown in my garden. One pot of this white flowing *Lobularia* grows into a plant over eighteen inches in diameter. Unlike the alyssum sold as seed or in six-packs, this hybrid stays low, tight, and flower-filled all season until hard frost. If you want a touch of white in your gardens for an evening wedding, you can't go wrong with Snow Princess. Note: this plant also does well in part shade. Just be sure it's getting at least three hours of direct sun and it will perform beautifully.

Salvia or Flowering Sage (*Salvia* species) Short, medium, or tall...blue, purple, or red...there's a variety of *Salvia* for just about every garden. In general, however, these annuals don't really get going until later in the summer, so don't plant them expecting lots of color in June.

Vinca or **Madagascar Periwinkle** (*Catharanthus roseus*) This is another plant that keeps getting better and better as new varieties are developed. Many types have flowers that resemble impatiens, but this annual does much better in full sun and hot climates. The flowers come in white, lavender, and a range of pink shades.

Marigolds (*Tagetes* species) In many parts of the world marigolds are traditional wedding flowers. They are strung into garlands or used in arrangements and bouquets, so why not in wedding landscapes as well? The bright yellow and orange flowers are particularly effective when mixed with other brilliant colors. They combine nicely with zinnias and are cooled down by blue *Ageratum*.

Annuals for Shade and Part Shade

Impatiens (*Impatiens wallerana*) I know that you see this annual everywhere, but it's ubiquitous for good reason. Plant impatiens in loosened soil with some organic fertilizer and they become a flower factory. Give them some synthetic plant food and they become an even *larger* bloom works. Impatiens will also grow and bloom well in full sun as long as they are watered deeply and regularly. Note that this annual won't flower as profusely in deep shade. For areas that receive no direct sun, use begonias and caladiums.

New Guinea Impatiens (*Impatiens* x *hawkeri*) New Guinea impatiens produce larger flowers than the standard variety, but they need a bit more fertilizer and sun than the impatiens listed above. Be sure to put New Guinea impatiens where they will get about three hours of direct sun at any point in the day, and make sure the soil is loose and fertile.

Coleus (*Solenostemon scutellarioides*) Hybrids of this annual just keep getting better and better. Many of them now grow well in sun or shade and don't flower at all, so no pinching is needed for some varieties. On the other hand, common seed-grown types that are available in six-packs usually need the flowers pinched off through the season. If you want low-maintenance plants, buy some of the named varieties in small pots. Look for plants from Simply Beautiful (Ball Horticultural) or Proven Winners for great colors and ease of growth.

Begonias (*Begonia* species) There are many more varieties of begonias available than in the recent past and these plants do well in part or full shade. Be aware that those with really large flowers (often called non-stop begonias) do shed the old blooms. These fallen flowers can be slippery when stepped on. If you're planting in containers that are next to walkways, make sure to use begonias with smaller flowers – just to be on the safe side. There are many varieties with variegated foliage available as well. These add yellow or silver leaf colors to the garden, in addition to the colors of the flowers.

Caladiums (*Caladium* x *hortulanum*) These plants grow best once the weather is hot. That means garden centers don't typically sell them until well into the summer. They are a good choice for warm climates and their white or pink leaves are striking and tropical in appearance. They begin to die back once the nights are cool, so they are not a good choice for a fall wedding.

House Plants There are many common houseplants with variegated foliage that are beautiful when planted outdoors in shade gardens. From spider plant to yellow-leaved *Schefflera*, these plants add foliage color and texture when used in deep shade gardens. To make things easy, they can be sunken into the ground while left in their pots. They can then be pulled up after the wedding, or in the fall, and brought back indoors. Another option is to give them to members of the wedding party, or other friends, as a remembrance of the day.

Ferns are usually easy to find and they do well on dark porches, the north side of houses, and other deep shade locations. A border of Boston ferns, for example, can instantly dress up bare foundations or shady pathways.

Perennials

If it's the week before the wedding and you're looking for eleventh-hour flowers for the garden, perennials might not be out of the question. Go to your local garden center and see what's in bloom. Some nurseries stock large perennial plants that are in full flower. As long as these aren't going by, they could be planted to provide color in the garden.

Be sure that the perennial you choose is right for your landscape, however. If the plant in question is a garden thug that spreads quickly and is hard to get rid of, you don't want it, flowers or not. Similarly, if your garden is very shady and the perennials that are in flower grow best in full sun, don't waste your time and money. Perennials usually cost more than annuals. If the plant won't thrive where you've placed it, then choosing something that comes back is silly.

Some perennial plants are full in the pot, but many are not. If the point of putting more plants into the garden is to fill it with flowers than choosing a plant that is less than lush won't do the job. Don't be swayed by the fact that the plant might come back and bloom again in the future. Think of the wedding, not the long-term garden.

Last Minute Color

Despite all our best efforts, there are bound to be some areas in the garden that will need last minute attention. It's usually not difficult to add color to places where other plantings haven't done well, or to locations that were overlooked in your advance tours of the property. If you have a well-stocked garden center nearby, you should be able to purchase larger plants that can be put into place within a few days before the wedding.

Small plants won't make much of an impact when providing last minute color. The best approach is to find the largest annuals or perennials that you can, and buy them already in bloom. Larger pots are faster to install as well, so you'll spend less time digging.

If your local nursery stocks hanging baskets of annuals, these are perfect for creating an instant flowerbed. Most hanging baskets are in full bloom at the time of sale. The plants can either be taken out of the hangers and placed in the ground, or the full baskets used as is.

Be they annuals or perennials, remember to water all newly added plants regularly. Since they'll have a root system the size of the pot they'll dry out more quickly than established plants. In the flurry of the days before the wedding these newly placed plants might be forgotten.

Assign someone the task of watering these plants in the period between the installation and the wedding itself. If you're in a very hot climate they may need watering every day. In cooler areas every three days will probably be adequate.

Chapter 6
Creative Containers and
Beautiful Baskets

Containers filled with flowers aren't just beautiful: for a garden wedding they can be functional as well. Urns of flowers or branches can be used to create a frame around, or archway over, the bride and groom. Large pots and urns can be used to attractively block areas where you don't want guests to walk, drive, or park. Pots can also delineate paths, cover tripping hazards, and decorate the entrance to Porta-Potties.

Containers can either be planted well in advance of your event, or assembled just days before the wedding. If you've had good luck with container plants in the past, by all means pot up annuals using colors that will compliment the garden, and then tend them until the big day. If your thumb tends to be more black than green, however, purchase your boxes, urns, and pots shortly before the wedding. Make sure to get good instructions about keeping the plants alive.

Some garden centers will plant your containers for you, so those who are limited on time or plant savvy might want to explore this option. Occasionally a nursery will be willing to accept your containers early in the season, plant them up, and then tend the arrangement until just before the event.

Many landscape companies have container services as well. This is another option for getting your pots, window boxes, and urns filled early in the season and kept in good shape. The landscape company may come weekly to remove wilted flowers, fertilize, and even replace a plant or two if that's what's needed.

Types of Containers

In addition to the classic types of pots and planters, you could choose to plant other vessels that are meaningful to the bride or groom, or appropriate to the theme of the wedding. A child's wagon, old suitcases, pots and pans, handbags, boots, or shoes can all be used as containers for plants. Anything that you want to keep in good shape should be lined with plastic and potted up right before the wedding. The flowers should then be removed soon after the event. This way you'll have minimal risk of water damage to the container.

If you're filling small containers with flowers, consider grouping three, five, or seven of them together into an arrangement rather than placing them singly in the garden. Unusual containers can also be placed among more traditional pots and boxes.

Plant the Furniture

Birdbaths are lovely when planted with flowering plants or fresh greenery. Even lawn or garden furniture can be filled. This can be a delightful way to handle chairs or benches that might look charming in the garden but aren't structurally suitable for actual sitting.

To turn a chair, bench, or small table into an instant planter, find a cardboard box that fits nicely on the seat or tabletop. Cut the sides down to five inches tall and line the inside with a plastic garbage bag. Cover the outer sides with sheet moss (available at any store that sells craft or floral supplies) glued onto the cardboard.

Wait until a couple of days before the wedding before you fill the box with dirt and flowering plants. For best results you can really cram the box with plants. This will give you a full, established look. You can also place small pots of ivy that trail over the edges, if desired. You can either use a mix of varieties or one type of plant throughout the box.

Water sparingly, just enough to keep the plants alive, but not so much that you fill the plastic-lined box with water. This type of planting is temporary, designed to be taken apart after the wedding. If you want a similar container that will last more than a week or two, use a sturdier pot or wooden box with drainage holes so the plants won't be kept too wet.

Hanging Baskets

Flowers spilling out of hanging baskets are wonderful accents for under porch eves, dressing up garage entrances, or the sides of buildings and fences. Decide in advance if you want such hangers to be all the same, and plan accordingly. If you need several that are the same color be sure to check with your local garden center well in advance; they can tell you if it's necessary to place a special order.

Should you decide to pot up your own hanging baskets, buy two or three extra containers and enough plants to fill them. This would be especially useful if you want all of the baskets to be the same; it wouldn't be unusual to have one or more of your carefully tended containers go downhill or die before the wedding. Put together a few extra baskets and be just like the grounds keepers at Disney World: you'll have a double that can be put in place anywhere it's needed. If it turns out these extra "emergency" baskets aren't needed, they can be planted in the ground or placed in other containers just before the event.

Note that if you're purchasing hanging baskets more than a month before the wedding, make sure they aren't already fully grown and in bloom. A basket of petunias that is already draping a foot over the edge and in full flower in May isn't likely to be so beautiful in August, for example. Any hanging basket that's fully mature early in the summer may not last into August or September.

If you fall in love with a particular hanging basket, be sure to ask someone knowledgeable if the plant you've selected will be attractive and in bloom for the wedding. Geraniums (*Pelargoniums*), *Scaevola, Begonias, Impatiens,* and *Mandevilla* all hold up very well and are likely to still be blooming – provided they've been kept watered and fertilized throughout the season.

Last Minute Alternatives

If you notice that your baskets or other containers have gone downhill before the wedding, there are alternatives – even if your garden center has long ago sold out of flowering annuals. Houseplants are usually available twelve months a year; pots or baskets of ferns, ivy, or other greenery can be as beautiful as blossoms. If you decide to fill containers with these types of greenhouse plants, do it at the last minute. It's important to wait because shade loving plants, like ferns, can get sunburned.

Emergency Containers, Non-Living

Occasionally it happens. Flowering plants in pots, window boxes, or hangers dry up, or they're destroyed by bugs, storms, or disease. There are no guarantees when it comes to the natural world. Fortunately, there are attractive alternatives for empty urns and other containers. Consider some of these last-minute fillers:

Cut flowers Sink wet floral foam (Oasis) into the soil and insert branches of foliage cut from the yard. Once the greenery is in place, add cut flowers. Be sure to put the flowers in place at the last possible minute, especially if they will be in the sun during the wedding. Spray them with florist's sealant to help keep them from wilting.

Pine Cones Piles of pinecones are lovely and especially appropriate if the wedding is in the fall.

Branches Gather an assortment of twigs, branches, and sticks. Once they've been collected, spear them into your pots or boxes. The more varieties, the better. If they're coated with lichens or mosses, that's wonderful. Short, medium, and tall – use them all.

Glass You might not have the means to fill your containers with a Dale Chihuly installation, but you can take a hint from this world-class artist and fill your boxes and pots with glass, glass, glass. Blown glass balls, figurines, dishes, and vases – using a variety is good. Winding some strands of white lights in and among these objects will make them come alive at night. Be creative. Here's a tip for making it all come together attractively: have something that is constant about all the glass objects chosen. It could be that all are round, clear, or blue. One unifying characteristic is enough, be it color, shape, or the object's use. For example, if every glass piece is a kitchen tool or wine glass, that will unify the entire display.

Rocks, Seashells, and Moss Place a mound of local stones in your empty urns or window boxes and you instantly have a modern, pleasing arrangement that also has a sense of place. If you're near the ocean, use seashells instead. Do you live in the woods? Stack up moss-covered pieces of bark and braches. It's all about celebrating where you are by using the materials at hand.

Chapter 7
Arches, Arbors, and Chuppahs

Some gardens may already have arches and arbors in place. If you're planning a garden wedding in a space that's already blessed with one of these structures, you should certainly make use of it. However, if your garden does not already have such a wonderful feature, there are many possibilities for creating one.

There are numerous options for making a ceremonial structure. You can purchase pre-made arches or arbors of metal or wood, or you can construct something yourself. Any of these options is fine, as long as the size is right and the structure is well secured. Make sure to note the measurements before ordering an arch. In fact, it's a good idea to go so far as putting stakes in the ground where it will be placed. This will help you judge if the size of the arbor is right for the garden, and if it's roomy enough to accommodate the bride and groom.

Most structures will need to either be anchored into the ground or placed into heavy containers. Even a temporary arch or arbor needs to be sturdy enough to withstand things like the wind, someone leaning against it, or something bumping into it. Upright poles can be set into holes in the ground or cement in large flowerpots.

Bamboo or birch poles lashed together with waxed cord can be used to form the canopy. An Internet search for "birch wedding chuppah poles" and "lashing cord for bamboo" will lead to sources for these materials. It's easy to hide the supporting base and pole ends set in cement-filled pots. On the wedding day simply wet a block (or appropriately sized amount) of Oasis floral foam and place it on top of the pots. Next add fresh flowers arranged to hide the cement.

In place of an arbor, large pots can be filled with branches and flowering plants to create drama at an entrance or where the ceremony will take place. If the branches are eight to ten feet high, and are placed in heavy metal or ceramic urns, they can be bent toward each other and tied together to create an arch. This twig arch can be left plain or decorated with fresh or paper flowers, ivy, garlands, or ribbons.

Rather than using pots filled with cement as the arbor base, you can also use pots or urns filled with living plants. The first step is to add moist potting soil to the pots or urns you'll be using. Next, firmly stick the arbor poles or branches into the centers of the pots and then water them in. Place the flowering annuals or foliage plants into the soil within just a few days before the wedding. Water after planting and also when the soil is dry.

If the pots or urns are going to be under a tent, fill them with soil and create the arch or add the chuppah poles after the containers are in place. Add plants or cut flowers the day before the wedding so that they'll be at their peak for the ceremony. Tents are often erected several days before the event. If the containers are planted a week ahead of time, there likely won't be enough light reaching the plants to keep them looking their best for that length of time.

Softening the Arch with Flowers

When designing arches, arbors, or chuppahs, most people envision them covered with flowering vines or climbing roses. This may or may not be possible to accomplish. It depends on how much lead time you have before the wedding, the time of year the ceremony will be held, and the climate where you live.

Climbing roses and most perennial vines take a few years to cover an arbor, and most of them don't bloom continually all summer. Annuals can take three to five months to climb up a structure as well, so new arches and arbors aren't likely to be vine covered for an early summer wedding. If the event is at the end of the summer or in the early fall, however, fast growing annuals can be the answer. Given fertilizer and sunny summer weather, hyacinth bean (*Dolicos lab-lab*), black-eyed Susan vine (*Thunbergia*), *Mandevilla* vine, and cardinal climber (*Ipomoea sloteri*) could all grow to the top of a seven-foot tall arbor.

For events held early in the season it might be necessary to tie garlands, bouquets of flowers, or foliage bunches to the arbor uprights. Tie them with long ribbons to create a softening and festive look. Another option is to visit your local craft or floral supply store. Many of them sell floral foam in plastic cages which can be wired or screwed onto the arbor. These cages then make it easy to place fresh flowers on any part of the structure.

Some gardens already have structures that are covered with climbing roses or other vines, but these plants may not be in bloom when the event takes place. There are several last-minute ways to add color in these cases including poking fresh flowers directly into the foliage, attaching bouquets to the uprights, and adding bows, ribbons, or origami. Stems of fresh flowers can be put into small plastic floral tubes that hold water. Using these will ensure that the blossoms stay fresh, even if they're added into the greenery the night before the wedding. These tubes can be purchased from florists or online from floral supply and craft stores.

Other possible decorations for garden structures include strings of fairy lights, paper lanterns, and bells. Craft supply stores often sell artificial branches with lights attached and short light strands that are battery operated. LED tea lights can be effective as well. A flat-topped arch might be lit with assorted pieces of milk glass, for example, each containing an LED tea light. Look for the varieties of LED lights that have a flickering, yellowish light if you want these to look like real candle flames. Secure the milk glass onto the arbor using pieces of florist sticky clay or sticky-backed Velcro.

Chapter 8
Wedding Flowers from Your Garden

For some, the garden will be the venue where the wedding is held and no more. In these cases, the goal is to be sure that the garden is a lovely environment for the festivities. Others want to use flowers from the garden for some or all of the wedding bouquets and arrangements. If your desire is to use as many garden grown flowers in the wedding as possible, extra blossoms may need to be grown. This will give you plenty to work with in creating the floral arrangements while leaving a good amount of color in the garden.

If you have a large property and know about an upcoming wedding more than two years in advance, you can plant a cutting garden of annuals and perennials to use in the arrangements. As mentioned earlier in the book, however, be sure to plant a variety of perennials that flower at different times since weather can delay or accelerate bloom times. Most cutting gardens need to be situated in an area that receives at least six hours of full sunshine, so be sure that such flowerbeds are placed in the right location.

When growing wedding flowers be sure to have a diversity of plants for cutting. One type of plant may not survive well because of the weather, for example, so it's good to have a few alternatives. Annuals that are grown from seed can vary from plant to plant; they're sometimes mislabeled or not pictured accurately for color. So if there's a color theme for the wedding you'll be safer if you also grow some possible substitutions. Plant what you think you need and then a third again extra. When it comes to flowers, more is usually better.

Supplemental Flowers

Unless the wedding flowers are fairly simple, it might be necessary to supplement garden grown blossoms with those purchased commercially. Local florists, supermarkets, and online direct-ship wholesale flower markets can be your source for these extra flowers. They can also provide varieties that you might not be able to grow. To this end, it's a good idea to create sample bouquets and arrangements in advance. This will help you judge which flowers might come from the garden and which might need to be purchased.

Roses are wedding flower favorites and are available from all the sources listed above. If you need more than a dozen, it might be less expensive to order them online. Other filler flowers that mix well with familiar garden-grown blooms include *Lisianthus, Trachelium* and *Bouvardia.*

In addition to flowers, greenery will be needed for arrangements and bouquets. Many common plants can be used for this purpose. Two or three weeks before the wedding make sure to cut test sprigs and place them in water or floral foam. This way you can evaluate your choices to make sure they'll last at least three days without wilting.

Ferns and *Hosta* are frequently used perennial choices; shrubs such as *Spirea, Rhododendron,* or willows work well for greening vases or bouquets.

Greens can also be purchased or even collected from roadsides. For example, I used wild heath aster foliage for a September wedding held in my garden. This greenery made a very successful, fine-textured filler. When collecting from roadsides, however, be sure you're not picking on private property or cutting protected or endangered plants. Also keep an eye out for plants such as poison ivy or poison oak. Being covered with a red, itchy rash shouldn't be part of any wedding.

Keeping Flowers Fresh

Be sure all garden flowers have been regularly watered *before* cutting so that they're already well hydrated when collected. Water your cutting garden in the same way you water your general landscaping by watering deeply every few days, or weekly if appropriate. This is the best practice and produces the cleanest flowers and foliage.

Cut the flowers in the morning then strip all leaves from the stems. After the leaves have been removed, immediately place the flowers into clean buckets filled with warm water and floral preservative. Floral preservatives are also called "flower food." They contain ingredients that inhibit stem-clogging microbes and also make the water more acidic for easier absorption.

Next, place the buckets of flowers in a cool place. This is important because flowers last longer when kept cold. In fact, an air conditioned room is ideal for storing flowers and creating arrangements. Commercial flower growers store freshly cut flowers at about 35 F, but it's unlikely that most homeowners have a place that can be kept at this low temperature.

Small amounts of flowers can be stored in an average refrigerator; larger amounts can be stored in a room cooled as much as possible by the air conditioning. Don't store flowers in a refrigerator where fruits and vegetables are kept. Many of these release ethylene gas, which will cause cut flowers to wilt.

Also note that some air conditioners seize up when the thermostat is set too low. Make sure to read the equipment manual, or consult a professional in heating and cooling equipment, before setting temperatures below 65 F.

Speeding Them Up and Slowing Them Down

No matter how carefully you've prepared, it's almost a given that the weather won't cooperate with your cut flower planning. It frequently happens that an unusually cold or warm season will either suppress or accelerate the normal blooming of the plants you've been counting on for the wedding. If this happens to you, don't despair. Although we can't hasten bloom in the landscape, or stop the garden flowers from opening ahead of schedule, there are ways that cut flowers can be delayed or forced into opening.

Warm weather may threaten to bring your planned wedding flowers into bloom prematurely. If this happens try slowing them down by picking them in bud and putting them in the refrigerator. Peony buds will hold this way when they're wrapped in newspaper and placed in a plastic bag. That's right, without their stems being in water! Other flowers last longer in a bucket of water mixed with floral preservative.

Take the chilled buds out the day before the wedding, make a fresh cut to the stems, and then put them back into warm water. Most blossoms will open quickly at that point. Be sure to spray them with florist's sealant once they open so that they don't lose much moisture and wilt quickly.

Just as warmer weather can speed blossoming, cooler weather can retard it. If you're counting on particular flowers for the wedding and the plants aren't yet budded, there isn't much you can do to hasten the production. However, if the flower buds are there but aren't open yet, you might try this technique. Pick the stems and put them immediately into buckets of warm water. Next, place these buckets of flowers in a warm room. Leave them there for a day before you begin working on the arrangements. The buds should continue to open and can also be used in arrangements as is.

Grasses, Branches, and Berries

When surveying your garden for bouquet components, don't stop at the greenery and flowers. Landscapes are filled with interesting arrangement materials and many of these can make a bouquet or centerpiece visually come alive.

Grasses can be wonderful with flowers, be they ornamental varieties that were purposefully planted or weeds that flourish on the property lines. Harvest grass plumes along with the flowers and treat their stems the same way.

Sprays of fruit can be pleasing when used in centerpieces. If you have elderberry, *Viburnum*, hawthorn, winterberry holly, or crabapple in your landscape, cut some of the fruiting branches the week before the wedding and see how they hold up. Even the green or black berries from pokeweed can be attractive in arrangements.

Branches are also wonderful for creating large floral arrangements and they can be especially effective in large reception areas. In the springtime, pussy willow, *Forsythia*, or any branches just breaking dormancy can look gorgeous when bursting out of very tall, clear vases. In the fall, those same large vases could be filled with winterberry holly or even bare branches covered with mosses or lichen.

Starting Early

Most garden flowers can be cut and arranged two to three days before the event. But again, testing a few stems in advance is always a good idea. Previously used vases and other flower vessels can be cleaned with bleach ahead of time. Supplies such as florist foam, waterproof tape, wire, stem wrapping, floral preservatives, spray sealant, and ribbons should be purchased well in advance.

If you have very specific flowers in mind, like a special color of roses, make sure to do your research at least a month in advance. Contact local florists or do online research to find the best pricing. Place your orders at least two weeks in advance, and have flowers delivered three or four days prior to the wedding. If the event is on Saturday, for example, have the flowers delivered Wednesday or Thursday so you have time to get them well hydrated before creating your arrangements.

The following schedule has helped me prepare the flower arrangements for a Saturday wedding.

Tuesday: Clean all buckets, vases, bowls, and other vessels you'll be using. Assemble all your tools and supplies. Prepare a work area with a tarp on the floor and a long table to work on.

Wednesday: Cut greens and place them in buckets of water. Cut blocks of floral foam to fit into containers, and then soak them if necessary. Secure the foam in the vases and bowls using transparent floral tape. Add greens to the containers that are going to be used for table arrangements. You can do this particular step either today or Thursday, depending on the number of arrangements to be made. If you're not using wet floral foam, use transparent waterproof tape to create a grid over the top of any container that's more than three inches across. This grid will be invisible once the flowers are finished but will hold all elements in place.

Thursday: Cut all garden flowers in the morning and place them in buckets of warm water mixed with flower food. Make fresh cuts on purchased flowers and place them in buckets of warm water as well. Add greens to vases and bowls if you haven't done this already. If you'll be making a large number of table arrangements, you might start assembling them as well.

Friday: Finish all table arrangements. Make boutonnieres and corsages, place them in loose plastic bags, then store them in the refrigerator. If there is time, do the bridesmaids' and bride's bouquets. You can use either florist foam bouquet holders, or you can place the ends of hand-tied bouquets in vases of water. Spray all finished arrangements with floral sealant.

Saturday: Finish any bouquets not yet assembled. Add flowers to chuppahs, arbors, or other outdoor structures. Flowers that will be in the sun should not be placed outdoors until the very last minute possible. Even if they are in plastic tubes filled with water or wet floral foam, they are likely to wilt when exposed to direct sunshine.

Garden Flowers with a Professional's Touch

Another alternative to arranging your own garden flowers is to ask a professional florist to work with materials from your garden. Some may not be willing use homegrown blooms, but others may welcome the opportunity. Just don't spring this on someone at the last minute.

If you're interested in having a professional help with the arrangements, contact them well in advance. Together you'll be able to work out details like which flowers you're likely to have in bloom and who will do the picking. Be in touch with the florist two weeks before the wedding to confirm which flowers will be out and then repeat this contact a week before the event. Most florists will need at least a week's advance notice if they have to buy extra flowers to supplement what you're anticipating from the garden.

Chapter 9
Embellishments

Part of the fun of planning a garden wedding is adding the small decorative touches that visually enhance the day. There are some pitfalls to watch for when planning for embellishments, however, so this chapter contains suggestions for trimming and adornment plus some words of caution about planning too much. As with so many aspects of wedding planning, advanced planning will serve you well.

A Theme and a Plan

Let's face it, it's easy to get carried away. When you know a wedding or rehearsal dinner will be taking place on your property, it's easy to make a variety of purchases in advance because "it will look good for the wedding." Some impulse buys might provide the perfect wedding décor, but others could just make the garden look cluttered or end up not being used at all. In order to avoid gathering a closet full of miscellaneous junk, it's smart to start out with a theme and a plan.

The theme of a wedding can be a color, location, season, flower, or the special interests of the bride and groom. While weddings of the past were usually all white affairs, today anything goes. Most couples want to have a celebration and ceremony that is personal to them. This approach provides the overall theme for many weddings. Use this, along with your preferences about color, flowers, etc., to guide your choice of embellishments.

In addition to having a general plan, keep in mind that time and energy will be stretched to the limits on the big day. Some ornamentation of the wedding site can be done ahead of time, but other items must be added at the last minute. Wrapping a tree trunk with small white lights can be accomplished the weekend before the wedding, for example, but hanging paper lanterns is best done the day of the event.

When making arrangements for the wedding décor, it will be useful to keep a schedule for installing the various elements. Delegating some of the last minute decorating tasks will probably be a necessity. If you have a wedding planner, he or she will take care of this scheduling. But if you're coordinating the event yourself, you'll need to orchestrate the installation of all the décor.

That said, here are some ideas for creating a magical landscape using materials beyond the plants and flowers.

Ribbons

Ribbons can be endlessly useful for a garden wedding. Long streamers can be hung from the branches of trees to create a more intimate or festive space. Large bows can be placed on arbors, fences, or around tree trunks. Bows with long streamers can be attached to the poles of reception tents; smaller, matching bows can then be tied to all chairs along the aisle where the ceremony is held.

Ribbons can also be useful for crowd control. A span of ribbon running between stakes that are ornamented with bows is a pretty way of saying, "Don't walk down this path," or "This area is off limits." On the other hand, a ribbon looped from stake to stake is an easy way to mark a path. For example, this can let guests know that the festivities, or the Porta-Potties, can be reached by traveling on a particular route.

Lights

From small tea lights to large paper lanterns, lights alone can define a party. Lights can be used to decorate everything – from the entry pathway coming off the street to the reception tables. Battery operated tea-lights are especially useful because they can illuminate a variety of objects and spaces. Tea-lights can be placed in vases, paper bags, and flower arrangements, or they can be used in the landscape as is. These small LED lights come with white or yellow-tinted "flames" that are either steady or flickering.

Most LED tea-lights last longer than 48 hours, allowing you to set them in place early in the day and turn them on before the festivities start. As night falls they will already be making their magic. Use the majority of these lights in areas where people will be walking or gathered after dark.

Although it's possible to find strings of small white lights that are battery operated, most "fairy lights" use electricity. Plan on using the majority of this type of lighting where an extension cord can provide the power. Because these lights are most abundant and inexpensive at Christmas time, smart wedding planners will buy them by the dozen in early December – even when planning for an August event.

Local craft stores or online sources offer artificial branches that are lit by battery powered LED lights. Plastic or paper orbs are available as well; these can be placed around the garden or along paths. They are illuminated with vase lighting, and can be remotely programed to glow in a range of different colors.

Paper Lanterns, Fans, and Parasols

Battery run LED lights are especially useful for making paper lanterns, fans, and parasols glow. These decorations can also be lit with traditional large or small string lights. They can be and hung as cascading groups (each placed at a different height), and positioned in clusters or in rows. Lanterns, fans, or parasols can be used in tents, on porches, under arbors, or hung from the branches of trees.

Paper parasols and weighted lanterns can even be placed along the ground to mark a path, or used as accents along the perimeter of a tent or garden. Place parasols on edge with the tops facing toward where people will be walking or gathered. Fix them in place by securing the handle ends to the ground using a piece of stiff wire bent into the shape of a large bobby pin.

Candles

Although LED lights are convenient and safe, some people find that nothing matches the magic created by real candles. Large pillar candles can be placed as is in a garden, or held above the plants on candelabras. Tea lights in votive candleholders can be beautiful as well. Be sure to position all real candles carefully to avoid catching mulch, plants, or clothing on fire.

In addition to concerns about safety, the disadvantage of real candles is that they need to be lit at the last minute. Although LED lights can be turned on in the morning or early afternoon and left untended, this doesn't work with real flames. Someone will need to light candles right before the ceremony or reception. It's also smart to put one or two people in charge of making sure that all candles are extinguished at the end of the festivities. The candle that was harmless when it was lit well above the mulch can turn into a hazard once it burns down near such flammable materials later in the night.

Bells

Tissue paper wedding bells used to be a standard party store offering, but real bells are better when it comes to decorating gardens. Use strings of brass bells hung from trees, bells strung on ribbons, or large temple bells to ornament arbors. Collections of bells are pretty when they're hanging from arbors or tied onto branches.

If you don't have a bell collection, make one in honor of the occasion. Ask each guest to bring a bell and hang them on ribbons to "ring in good fortune" for the bride and groom. Tie the ribbons where you want the bells to hang. Maybe even start things off by attaching bells that have been collected at a bridal shower or from the happy couple's families.

Remember the expression, "We'll be there with bells on." It signifies how delighted we are to celebrate. Put another way, bells can also be used to help remember those who aren't in attendance. You can suggest that people who are unable to attend might send a small bell for the décor; this would be a symbol that they are there in spirit. Bells can also be hung to represent significant family members who have passed away but would have been delighted to celebrate the marriage.

Baskets

Because baskets are both woven and receptacles, they can symbolize the weaving and gathering together of two families and many traditions. They are also a budget-conscious way to decorate. Many people have an assortment of baskets already, or they can find inexpensive ones at garage sales and thrift shops.

When used with plastic liners, available at garden centers and craft stores, baskets can hold flowers for the table arrangements. Baskets can also be used to light the garden. Just fill them with several LED tea lights and place them among the plants. You can also fill baskets with pinecones, flower petals, herbs, rocks, or seashells and use them throughout the wedding to inexpensively provide a decorative sense of place.

Place "prayer baskets" or "good wishes baskets" in various places where the ceremony, cocktails, and reception will be held. Provide paper and pens then invite guests to write a prayer, wish, or message for the bride and groom. The messages can then be opened after the ceremony or on the couple's first anniversary.

Baskets can also be filled with a combination of potpourri and fresh flowers from the wedding. Place them in Porta-Potties or anywhere else that sweet scents would be appreciated. At the end of the evening some of the flowers from various arrangements could be added to these baskets and allowed to dry naturally, providing long-lasting mementos for the bridal party or guests.

Petals

Flower petals have traditionally been scattered down the aisle by the flower girl. But why stop there? Petals can be used to define spaces throughout a garden wedding. Scatter them where the ceremony will take place, along pathways, or use different colors to delineate separate areas such as the ceremony site, cocktail area, or the reception location.

Gather petals from the garden or recycle the broken blooms and outer petals left over from cleaning up purchased roses. If collecting petals a day or two in advance, place them in a loosely closed plastic bag (don't "zip lock" it completely) and store them in the refrigerator to keep them fresh. Large quantities of rose petals can also be purchased from online, direct-ship flower sources.

A Sense of Place

A garden wedding has an automatic sense of place built in. The ceremony is special because it's taking place in the outdoors. All décor normally associated with gardens and gardening is automatically appropriate. Flower pots, watering cans, benches, birdbaths, and other garden ornaments can be used seamlessly for garden weddings.

Use flower pots to hold candles, or place a grouping of terracotta pots upside down to elevate candles among plants in the garden. Fill the birdbath with flowers, seashells, or other items that are meaningful to the bride and groom. Hang watering cans from ribbons tied to a large arbor instead of hanging bells or flowers. In fact, those watering cans could contain flower arrangements so that blossoms spill from the hanging cans. You could do the same thing by placing the cans on patios, decks, or porches.

In addition to normal gardening objects, every region of the country has things that are special to that area. Many people like to include these objects in an outdoor wedding. Seashells and driftwood when near the seaside, cacti when in the desert, or other items that are particular to your region – local objects fit really well with a garden wedding.

Group Your Embellishments

The general rule for designing with garden ornaments applies to wedding trappings as well: groups are more effective than placing one here and one there. Instead of spacing pillar candles five or ten feet apart, for example, group three to five of them together in a prominent location. Strategically clustering the decorations together will create more festive surroundings.

Chapter 10
After the Ball

One advantage of a home garden wedding is that
nothing has to be cleared away at the end of the evening.
Unlike an event that is held in a rented hall, the flower
arrangements and other decorations can be left in place to
be dealt with the next day. Aside from the usual post-
wedding cleanup, however, there are some things worth
doing after the big day has come and gone.

Lawn Repair

If the weather has been dry, water the lawn as soon as the chairs, tables, and other equipment have been picked up. Having a crowd repeatedly walk up and down the same areas of turf is very hard on it. A thorough watering will help it to recover.

Throughout the week after the wedding, you'll be likely to notice more damage to the turf. The wear and damage doesn't show up immediately. For example, there may be places where the caterers have emptied hot water from buffet pans, or spots where guests have spilled a drink. If you start to see dead patches a few days after the wedding, just water the areas well, rake up the browned grass, loosen the soil with a rake, and scatter grass seed over the area.

If many people have walked over the same area of lawn for a long time, it would also be a good idea to have the grass aerated. The best timing for this is in the fall, after the wedding. Compact soil isn't turf-friendly, and your lawn will grow better the following season if the compaction is reduced.

When it comes to a stressed lawn, it's typical for people to think about fertilizing but ignore tasks such as aeration. In fact, the aeration is more vital. Depending on the time of year, applying fertilizer could actually be harmful. Fertilizer is more important in the spring and early fall than at any other time of the year. If your post-wedding period is in the heat of the summer, fertilizing would be a mistake.

With all plants it's hard to go wrong with a light application of organic fertilizer. Just be sure to avoid even this in extremely hot weather.

Scattering seed in bare areas can also be helpful after the big event. Again, this is best done in early summer or fall. Be sure to keep the seed and new grass moist while it's getting established.

Keeping it Beautiful

After creating such a lovely landscape for the wedding, you'll want to be sure that it remains attractive for as long as possible. Part of that effort is accomplished with proper watering.

There's a tendency for people to give a huge sigh of relief when an event is over, and then forget about what it takes to keep the plants in good shape. Remember that all plants that have been recently put into the ground will need watering at least once a week. Containers require a good soaking whenever they are dry. In areas of the country that are hot, new plants in the ground might need to be drenched twice a week and pots and boxes watered every day.

Plants still in pots that were placed directly into the garden will need more frequent watering than those planted in the soil. These can be left in place and tended, planted into the ground after the event, or used elsewhere.

Using the Garden For More Than the Wedding

Admit it. You've put a great deal of effort toward getting your landscape into shape for the wedding. So doesn't it seem kind of a shame that after the final flurry, in just one eventful day, something you've focused on is suddenly gone? Some people will be relieved and content to quietly enjoy their gardens for the rest of the season. But others might want to take advantage of how great it all looks, and be willing share it again.

Scheduling other events can be another way of taking full advantage of your efforts. For example, you might offer to host other parties or charity events in the garden. Extend the celebration: consider hosting a tea, auction, garden tour, or other fundraiser for a local non-profit.

Share the Wealth

After your garden wedding is over, I hope that you'll share your experiences with others. Consider writing a blog about your progress and posting photos of the wedding.

Stop by my garden wedding website, www.gardenweddingexpert.com, and click on the page titled "The Garden Lady's Wedding Tips" to read ideas and comments. If you send me some photos of your garden wedding I'll post them, with your permission, on the *Tips* blog.

I look forward to hearing from you, and congratulations!

Acknowledgements

It takes a village to produce a book, and I'm lucky to be supported and surrounded by so many encouraging friends, family, and knowledgeable professionals.

Although I'm indebted to so many, I must recognize by name the dear people who got married as I was finishing *A Garden Wedding*. During the summer when I was revising this manuscript, I was blessed to be a part of – and to celebrate at – the outdoor weddings of Simon Fornari and Rachel Snow, Kate Owens and Rusty Stacy, and Jesse Galdston and Maya Gomes. I wish you all many adventurous years together, and a preponderance of times as lovely and sparkling as the skies on your wedding days.

Betty Mackey, of B.B. Mackey Books, has my appreciation for being so informative about options for publishing and ways to create effective illustrations. Thanks also to Lauren Forest, The Word Perfectionist, for her careful and much needed polishing of my manuscript.

Most of all and once again, thanks to Dan Fornari, the dear man who stood with me in the first of many gardens we've planted together and said, "I do." I did then and I do now.

Index

CPSIA information can be obtained at www.ICGtesting.com
Printed in the USA
LVOW07s1512250516

489934LV00022B/1187/P